MW00930435

Workbook

For

How To Know A

Person

The Art of Seeing Others Deeply and Being Deeply
Seen

(A Practical Guide to David Brooks' book)

By

Kee Notes

Copyright © 2023

Do not copy or transmit any part of this material without seeking the necessary publishing permissions.

INTRODUCTION

This book is a must-read for everyone who wants to live a fulfilling life as it delves into the art of seeing others and making them feel seen, heard, and understood. It also explores the importance of being seen, the reason why people don't see others, how we can see others, the power of attention, reasons why we need companionship, how circumstances can change a person, how to be a good conversationalist, and how and when to ask the right questions.

It highlights the need for relationships and the consequences of social disconnection, how to handle hard conversations, how to recognize and serve a friend in despair, and the art of empathy. It further discusses personality traits, stages of life tasks, how to make people share their life stories, what culture is, the importance of having a past or an ancestor, and the role they in making the world what it is today, and what wisdom is.

PART 1

I SEE YOU

CHAPTER ONE

The Power of Being Seen

Objectives

1. To understand the importance of upbringing in a person's lifestyle.

2. To explore the significance of living a detached life and the importance of living a social life.

3. To educate readers on the art of seeing others and making them feel seen, heard, and understood.

Summary

In this chapter, the author discusses his culture of upbringing, how it made him live a detached life, and how he was able to alter his life. It also talks about the significance of living a detached life, the need for social skills, what it entails, and how we can build our social skills. It further explores the importance of understanding what others go through as it is the most important social tool, the benefit of being seen and understood, and the concept diminisher and illuminator.

Lessons

1. Love must be expressed.

2. The culture of upbringing can affect a person's lifestyle.

3. It is bad to repress your emotions.

4. Life has a way of tenderizing people.

5. Living a detached life is a withdrawal from life, an estrangement not just from other people but from yourself.

6.Wise people don't just possess information; they possess a compassionate understanding of other people.

7. Being open-hearted is a prerequisite for being a full, kind, and wise human being.

8. The most important social skill is the ability to understand what another person is going through.

Questions

1. How can love be expressed and why should we express it?

_____

_____

_____

_____

_____

_____

_____

_____

_____

_____

_____

_____

_____

_____

2. What is the connection between a person's upbringing
   and his lifestyle?

_____

_____

_____

_____

_____

_____

_____

_____

_____

_____

_____

3. What are the consequences of repressing your emotions
   or feelings?

_____

_____

_____

_____

_____

_____

_____

_____

_____

_____

4. How can fear of intimacy, fear of vulnerability, and
   social ineptitude lead to repression of emotion?

_____

_____

_____

_____

_____

_____

_____

_____

_____

_____

_____

_____

5. Which detrimental outcomes are associated with living
   a detached life?

_____

_____

_____

_____

_____

_____

_____

_____

_____

_____

_____

6. Why do we need to have social skills, what does it entail and how can we build it?

_____

_____

_____

_____

_____

_____

_____

_____

_____

_____

7. Why is it important to understand what others are going through and how can we cultivate this skill?

_____

_____

_____

_____

_____

_____

_____

_____

_____

_____

_____

8. What are the benefits of being seen and understood by others?

_____

_____

_____

_____

_____

_____

_____

_____

_____

_____

9. What are the advantages and disadvantages of being a diminisher and an illuminator?

_____

_____

_____

_____

_____

_____

_____

_____

_____

_____

_____

10. How can we see others and make them feel seen, heard, and understood?

_____

_____

_____

_____

_____

_____

_____

_____

_____

_____

CHAPTER TWO

How Not to See a Person

Objectives

1. To explore and understand the reason why we don't see others.

2. To explore how we can break out of diminisher proclivities.

3. To highlight the effect of not seeing others in our everyday life.

Summary

This chapter is an exploration of the best ways to see people and the mechanisms that can be utilized by us for this purpose. The chapter also details attributes that can suppress our ability to actually see a person. Furthermore, the chapter examines concepts, such as self-centeredness, anxiety, naïve realism, lesser-minds problem, objectivism, and static mindset, and how these concepts influence our approach at seeing people.

Overall, the thesis of this chapter is an exploration and examination of the issues and associated concepts that affect our perception of people and it further offers methodical approaches that can help us manage these perceptions.

Lessons

1. Self-centeredness, anxiety, naïve realism, lesser-minds problem, objectivism, essentialism, and static mindset can lead you in to not seeing others.

2. Being able to appreciate the perspective of others is a social skill.

3. Objectivism is a terrible way to see a person but it is good for group surveys.

4. Each particular life is far more astounding and unpredictable than any of the generalizations scholars and social scientists make about groups of people.

5. If you want to understand humanity, you have to focus on the thoughts and emotions of individuals, not just data about groups.

6. Essentialists use stereotypes to categorize vast swaths of people.

7. Each person is a fathomless mystery.

8. You need to train hard to see people for who they are and how you can start seeing others.

Questions

1. What are the reasons why we don't see others?

_____

_____

_____

_____

_____

_____

_____

_____

_____

2. How can we appreciate the view of others and what are its benefits?

_____

_____

_____

_____

_____

_____

_____

_____

_____

_____

_____

3. What are the consequences of self-centeredness, anxiety, naïve realism, lesser-minds problem, objectivism, essentialism, and static mindset concerning this chapter?

_____

_____

_____

_____

_____

_____

_____

_____

_____

_____

4. How does being an essentialist make you not see others?

_____

_____

_____

_____

_____

_____

_____

_____

_____

_____

_____

5. What are the differences between lesser-minds problem and static mindset?

_____

_____

_____

_____

_____

_____

_____

_____

_____

_____

6. Why do we need to and how can we break out of diminisher proclivities?

_____

_____

_____

_____

_____

_____

_____

_____

_____

_____

7. Why should we use trained and not untrained eyes to see people?

_____

_____

_____

_____

_____

_____

_____

_____

_____

_____

8. About this chapter, what is the connection between seeing others and fierce attachment?

_____

_____

_____

_____

_____

_____

_____

_____

_____

_____

9. How can you love a person and yet not know the person?

_____

_____

_____

_____

_____

_____

_____

_____

_____

_____

_____

10. How can we stop being a diminisher?

_____

_____

_____

_____

_____

_____

_____

_____

_____

_____

_____

_____

_____

CHAPTER THREE

Illumination

Objectives

1. To recognize and understand the power of attention.

2. To explore the concept of illumination (seeing others in their fullness).

3. To highlight the importance of illuminating gaze and explore the features of the Illuminator's gaze.

Summary

This chapter explores the concept of illumination, why we are an illuminator, the power of attention, how we should treat people, the importance and function of the gaze, and the features of the Illuminator's gaze which are tenderness, active curiosity, affection, receptive ness, generosity, and holistic attitude.

Lessons

1. Every journalist has their interviewing style.

2. Each of us has a characteristic way of showing up in the world, a physical and mental presence that sets a tone for how people interact with us.

3. Your first gaze when you encounter people represents your posture towards the world.

4. The quality of your life depends quite a bit on the quality of attention you project out onto the world.

5. Being an illuminator is better than being a diminisher.

6. Greet and treat everyone with reverence and respect like Jimmy.

7. The shape of our knowledge becomes the shape of our living.

8. Tenderness, curiosity, affection, receptiveness, generosity, and holistic attitude can be seen in an illuminator's gaze.

Questions

1. Who and what drives civic life in your areas?

_____

_____

_____

_____

_____

_____

_____

_____

_____

_____

_____

2. Why should we be more like an illuminator than a diminisher?

_____

_____

_____

_____

_____

_____

_____

_____

_____

_____

3. How should we treat people that will be regarded as we are illuminating them?

_____

_____

_____

_____

_____

_____

_____

_____

_____

_____

_____

4. When practicing illuminationism, what should we do?

_____

_____

_____

_____

_____

_____

_____

_____

_____

_____

_____

_____

_____

_____

5. How is gaze significant to illumination in this chapter?

_____

_____

_____

_____

_____

_____

_____

_____

_____

_____

6. How can we overcome our insecurities and self-preoccupation and open ourselves up to the experience of another person?

_____

_____

_____

_____

_____

_____

_____

_____

_____

_____

_____

7. From your experience, how can you explain tenderness and relate it to this chapter?

_____

_____

_____

_____

_____

_____

_____

_____

_____

8. How can we become illuminators in our everyday life?

_____

_____

_____

_____

_____

_____

_____

_____

_____

_____

_____

9. What should we do for us to see beyond the cliche characters of people around us?

_____

_____

_____

_____

_____

_____

_____

_____

_____

10. What is morality and immoral act all about?

_____

_____

_____

_____

CHAPTER FOUR

Accompaniment

Objectives

1. To explore and recognize the importance of accompaniment.

2. To highlight the qualities and benefits of accompaniment and how it can help us see people.

3. To understand the effect of other-centeredness and self-centeredness in our everyday life.

Summary

This chapter talks about the importance of accompaniment, how it can help you know someone better or improve your relationship, the qualities of accompaniment like patience, playfulness, etc., and the benefits of accompaniment.

Lessons

1. Accompaniment involves getting used to or comfortable with each other.

2. Nothing can be heard in the mind until the situation feels safe and familiar to the body.

3. If you don't talk about the little things regularly, it's hard to talk about the big things even if you are familiar with that person.

4. Accompaniment is the ability to hold back and be aware of the other person's timetable.

5. Accompaniment is an other-centered way of moving through life.

6. Getting to know someone else is always going to be a vulnerable proposition so just go for it.

7. People are more fully human when they play.

8. Playfulness leads to spontaneous communication.

Questions

1. What is the need for accompaniment?

_____

_____

_____

_____

_____

_____

_____

2. According to the chapter, how can we relate patience to accompaniment?

_____

_____

_____

_____

_____

_____

_____

_____

_____

_____

3. What are the features of accompaniment?

_____

_____

_____

_____

_____

_____

_____

_____

_____

_____

4. Why is accompaniment necessary in getting to know a person?

_____

_____

_____

_____

_____

_____

_____

_____

_____

_____

5. How is playfulness significant to accompaniment?

_____

_____

_____

_____

_____

_____

_____

_____

_____

_____

_____

6. In what way can playfulness help us see people for who they are?

_____

_____

_____

_____

_____

_____

_____

_____

_____

7. What advantage does other-centeredness have over self-centeredness?

_____

_____

_____

_____

_____

_____

_____

_____

_____

_____

_____

8. What is the relationship between presence and accompaniment?

_____

_____

_____

_____

_____

_____

_____

_____

_____

_____

_____

9. Of what significance is accompaniment and its qualities to us in our everyday life?

_____

_____

_____

_____

_____

_____

_____

_____

_____

10. At which point in your life has accompaniment helped you pull through?

_____

_____

_____

_____

_____

_____

_____

CHAPTER FIVE

What Is a Person?

Objectives

1. To explore the question, "What is a person?"

2. To recognize the way circumstances can change a person and how people react to the same situation differently.

3. To educate readers on the subjective and objective reality.

Summary

This chapter talks about how everybody experiences the same circumstances differently using the story of Carrère, Hélène, Delphine, Jérôme, and Ruth as examples. It also talks about how a person's life history can affect how he reacts to situations, subjective and objective reality, how our whole perspective, our way of seeing, interpreting, and experiencing the world can be transformed, and exposes the flaws of our way of seeing things.

Lessons

1.Events happen in our lives, but each person processes and experiences any given event in their unique way.

2. Your life history can affect how you react to situations.

3. Experience is not what happens to you, it's what you do with what happens to you.

4. There are two layers of reality which are objective and subjective reality.

5. Our well-being depends less on what happens but on how we deal with the situation.

6. Our way of seeing and experiencing things can be changed.

7. People don't see the world with their eyes; they see it with their entire life.

8. The model we choose to use to understand something determines what we find.

Questions

1. How can people can experience the same event in different ways?

_____

_____

_____

_____

_____

_____

_____

_____

_____

_____

_____

2. What is the difference between objective and subjective reality and how does it affect the way we react to or experience events in our lives?

_____

_____

_____

_____

_____

_____

_____

_____

3. Why is it significant to view things from other people's perspectives?

_____

_____

_____

_____

_____

_____

_____

_____

_____

_____

4. How can we change our way of seeing, interpreting, and experiencing things?

_____

_____

_____

_____

_____

_____

_____

_____

_____

_____

_____

_____

5. What effect does constructionism have on the way we experience the world?

_____

_____

_____

_____

_____

_____

_____

_____

6. How do perceive situations, experience moments, and construct reality?

_____

_____

_____

_____

_____

_____

_____

_____

7. How does perception work?

_____

_____

_____

_____

_____

_____

_____

_____

_____

8. Where or what are the flaws in the way we see things and how can they affect the way we experience moments and construct reality?

_____

_____

_____

_____

_____

_____

_____

_____

9. How do you construct your reality and make your life meaning?

_____

_____

_____

_____

_____

_____

_____

_____

_____

10. From the chapter, what can you say is a person?

_____

_____

_____

_____

_____

_____

CHAPTER SIX

Good Talks

Objectives

1. To explore what it's like to engage, to probe the deep recesses of another person's mind.

2. To understand and correct misconceptions about who a good conversationalist is.

3. To highlight strategies we can use to be a good conversationalist.

Summary

The chapter explores the importance of being a good conversationalist, who is a good conversationalist, misconception of who a good conversationalist is. It also highlights what a good conversation consists of, what it means, and ways to good conversationalist.

Lessons

1. Imagining what is in people's head won't work, if you are trying to know a person you have to talk to them.

2. Getting to know someone involves talking, listening and not just seeing.

3. A good conversationalist is a person who is capable of leading people on a mutual expedition toward understanding.

4. A good conversation is an act of joint exploration.

5. Paying attention when having a conversation with someone makes you a good conversationalist.

6. Everyone in a conversation is facing an internal conflict between self-expression and self-inhibition.

7. People like to talk about what they know and not unfamiliar things.

8. Being a good conversationalist improves your social skills.

Questions

1. What is it like to engage, to probe the deep recesses of another person's mind?

_____

_____

_____

_____

_____

_____

_____

_____

_____

_____

2. What is a good conversationalist like and how can we be a good conversationalist?

_____

_____

_____

_____

_____

_____

_____

_____

_____

3. How significant does being a good conversationalist have in helping you know a person?

_____

_____

_____

_____

_____

_____

_____

_____

_____

4. What is the difference between a good conversationalist and a lecturer?

_____

_____

_____

_____

_____

_____

_____

_____

5. What does a good conversation comprise and how do we have a good conversation?

_____

_____

_____

_____

_____

_____

_____

_____

_____

_____

6. How is being a good conversationalist a social skill?

_____

_____

_____

_____

_____

_____

_____

_____

7. How do we know that we are having a good convention with someone?

_____

_____

_____

_____

_____

_____

_____

_____

_____

_____

8. What are the benefits of being a good conversationalist?

_____

_____

_____

_____

_____

_____

_____

_____

9. From personal experience, what does it feel like to have someone actively listen to you?

_____

_____

_____

_____

_____

_____

_____

_____

_____

_____

10. According to the chapter, how can we make the speaker
an author instead of a witness?

_____

_____

_____

_____

_____

_____

_____

_____

_____

_____

_____

_____

CHAPTER SEVEN

The Right Questions

Objectives

1. To educate the reader on the importance of asking the right questions.

2. To highlight how we can ask the right questions.

3. To highlight what a good and bad question is made up of.

Summary

This chapter talks about the importance of asking the right questions, how we can ask the right questions and the consequences of asking the wrong questions. It also talks about what bad and good questions comprise.

Lessons

1. People answer better with narrative.

2. The average child asks about forty thousand questions between the ages of two and five.

3. Sometimes a broad, dumb question is better than a smart question, especially one meant to display how well-informed you are.

4. Questioning is a moral practice.

5. The worst kind of questions are closed questions and the ones that evaluate.

6. A question should be humble and open-minded.

7. People are longing to be asked questions about who they are as they want to be self-present.

8. People take more pleasure in sharing information about themselves than receiving money.

Questions

1. Why is it important to ask the right questions and what are the consequences of asking the wrong question?

_____

_____

_____

_____

_____

_____

_____

_____

_____

_____

_____

2. What is the connection between asking the right question and being a good conversationalist?

_____

_____

_____

_____

_____

_____

_____

_____

3. How can you explain this statement "Questioning is a moral practice" relating it to the chapter?

_____

_____

_____

_____

_____

_____

_____

_____

_____

4. What strategy should be used while asking questions?

_____

_____

_____

_____

_____

_____

_____

_____

_____

5. How do we ask and know the right questions to ask?

_____

_____

_____

_____

_____

_____

_____

_____

_____

_____

_____

_____

6. Is timing important while asking the right questions?

_____

_____

_____

_____

_____

_____

_____

_____

7. From your perspective, what do you consider as a bad and good question?

_____

_____

_____

_____

_____

_____

_____

_____

_____

_____

8. How does asking the right questions help you to become an illuminator?

_____

_____

_____

_____

_____

_____

_____

_____

9. From your point of view, do you think the statement "People take more pleasure in sharing information about themselves than receiving money" is true?

_____

_____

_____

_____

_____

_____

_____

_____

_____

_____

10. What is the effect of listening to people?

_____

_____

_____

_____

_____

_____

_____

_____

_____

_____

_____

_____

_____

_____

_____

PART 2

I SEE YOU IN YOUR STRUGGLES

CHAPTER EIGHT

The Epidemic of Blindness

Objectives

1. To highlight the importance of relationships.

2. To understand the consequences of social disconnection.

3. To see the epidemic of loneliness and meanness.

Summary

This chapter emphasizes the importance of relationships and the consequences of social disconnection. It also talks about the effect of politics on the modern world and what happens when you attempt to assuage your sadness, and loneliness through politics.

Lessons

1. We need relationships the most but we suck at it.

2. Social disconnection leads to ruinous and self-reinforcing.

3. People who are lonely and unseen become suspicious leading to self-loathing and self-doubt.

4. Sadness, lack of recognition, and loneliness turn into bitterness.

5. Pain that is not transformed can be transmitted.

6. Politics can turn lonely people into non-lonely people as it offers a sense of belonging.

7. Love rejected comes back as hatred.

8. The essence of evil is the tendency to obliterate the humanity of another.

Questions

1. How can we remedy the problems of our modern society?

_____

_____

_____

_____

_____

_____

_____

_____

2. What led to the increase in the suicide rate in the 21st century?

_____

_____

_____

_____

_____

_____

_____

_____

_____

3. Why do humans need relationships and what are the consequences of lack of it?

_____

_____

_____

_____

_____

_____

_____

_____

_____

_____

4. What strategy can we use to improve our relationship with others?

_____

_____

_____

_____

_____

_____

_____

_____

_____

5. In what way has modern society failed to stabilize relationships with others here by leading to social disconnection?

_____

_____

_____

_____

_____

_____

_____

_____

_____

_____

6. What are the consequences of social disconnection, and how can it be cured and prevented?

_____

_____

_____

_____

_____

_____

_____

_____

_____

7. What is the difference between spontaneous sociability and recognition order?

_____

_____

_____

_____

_____

_____

_____

_____

_____

_____

8. What is the effect of assuaging your sadness, and loneliness through politics?

_____

_____

_____

_____

_____

_____

_____

_____

9. What causes social disconnection, loneliness, and meanness?

_____

_____

_____

_____

_____

_____

_____

_____

_____

_____

10. Concerning the chapter, what is understood by the term moral formation, and what effect does it have on our modern world?

_____

_____

_____

_____

_____

_____

_____

_____

_____

_____

_____

CHAPTER NINE

Hard Conversations

Objectives

1. To understand how to handle hard conversations.

2. To highlight the things we should know before entering a hard conversation.

3. To understand the consequences of a hard conversation going south.

Summary

The chapter talks about how to handle hard conversations, what to say when to say it, and what not to say. It also emphasizes the need for us to prepare before having a hard conversation listing things you must know before entering a hard conversation. It further highlights the consequences of a hard conversation going bad and how we can redeem it.

Lessons

1. To have an in-depth knowledge of a person's characteristics, you have to see the person in front of you as a distinct individual.

2. Before entering into any hard conversation, it's important to think about conditions before you think about content.

3. Every conversation takes place on two levels namely official and actual conversation.

4. Every conversation exists within a frame.

5. Curiosity is the ability to explore something even in stressful and difficult circumstances.

6. A person who is lower in any power structure than you are has a greater awareness of the situation than you do.

7. Hard conversations are hard because people in different life circumstances construct very different realities.

8. There is no way to make hard conversations unheard.

Questions

1. What strategy can be used to know and understand a person?

_____

_____

_____

_____

_____

_____

_____

_____

_____

_____

2. Concerning this chapter, what do you understand by the term hard conversation?

_____

_____

_____

_____

_____

_____

_____

_____

_____

3. How do we handle hard conversations?

_____

_____

_____

_____

_____

_____

_____

_____

_____

_____

4. What are the things you must know before entering a hard conversation?

_____

_____

_____

_____

_____

_____

_____

_____

_____

_____

5. What is the difference between official and actual conversation?

_____

_____

_____

_____

_____

_____

_____

_____

_____

6. What happens when a hard conversation goes bad?

_____

_____

_____

_____

_____

_____

_____

_____

_____

7. How can we redeem a hard conversation that is going bad?

_____

_____

_____

_____

_____

_____

_____

_____

_____

8. How can splitting rectify a bad hard conversation?

_____

_____

_____

_____

_____

_____

_____

_____

_____

_____

9. Why is it necessary to have a hard conversation and what is the purpose for having it?

_____

_____

_____

_____

_____

_____

_____

_____

_____

10. How can we make a hard conversation easy?

_____

_____

_____

_____

_____

CHAPTER TEN

How Do You Serve a Friend Who Is in Despair?

Objectives

1. To understand and recognize what it means to be in despair.

2. To know how to serve a friend who is in despair.

3. To explore the concept of depression.

Summary

In this chapter, the author delves into depression, its causes, how to care for someone with depression, and what depression is all about using the story of his friend Pete who died of depression.

Lessons

1. Depression is not just emotion associated with sorrow, it is a state of consciousness that distorts perceptions of time, space, and self.

2. Depression is the malfunction of the instrument we use to determine reality.

3. Don't ask a depressed person about the cause of his depression.

4. Our wounds heal under the consoling words that only reveal the depths of pain.

5. Depression makes it hard to imagine a time when things will ever be better.

6. Don't try to coax a person out of depression, just be there for them.

7. Each mind constructs its reality but depression changes your perception of reality.

8. Depressed people see a world without pleasure.

Questions

1. Through the instrumentality of the nuggets seen in this chapter, how do you serve a friend who is in despair?

_____

_____

_____

_____

_____

_____

_____

_____

_____

_____

2. What Is the major cause of depression and how can it be stopped?

_____

_____

_____

_____

_____

_____

_____

_____

3. What practices should we use in our daily lives to prevent depression?

_____

_____

_____

_____

_____

_____

_____

_____

_____

_____

_____

4. Why is it significant to overcome depression, can't we live a normal life with it?

_____

_____

_____

_____

_____

_____

_____

_____

_____

5. Why is it essential for us to take care of people in despair?

_____

_____

_____

_____

_____

_____

_____

_____

_____

_____

_____

6. How does depression change your perception of reality?

_____

_____

_____

_____

_____

_____

_____

_____

_____

_____

_____

_____

7. Why does each mind construct its reality and it is possible for our perception of reality to overlap with those around us?

_____

_____

_____

_____

_____

_____

_____

_____

_____

_____

8. How can we make a depressed person feel heard and understood?

_____

_____

_____

_____

_____

_____

_____

_____

_____

_____

9. Why does the author emphasize the need for us to not coax a depressed person?

_____

_____

_____

_____

_____

_____

_____

_____

_____

10. Have you ever served a friend who is in despair, if yes, what was the outcome?

_____

_____

_____

_____

CHAPTER ELEVEN

The Art of Empathy

Objectives

1. To explore and understand the art of empathy.

2. To understand the effect of trauma on our present plot and trajectory of life.

3. To highlight the benefits and problems associated with building a defensive system.

Summary

This chapter discusses empathy which is the capacity or result of understanding a person from his point of view. It also talks about defenses that people put up that prevents them from further trauma, how upbringing can shape your future, the effect of trauma or wound in our daily and future life how trauma can be passed down from generation to generation, and the problems related with building a defense system. It further discusses the skills that trauma consists of which are mirroring, mentalizing, and caring, how emotions are created and the function of the body in creating emotions, how to measure how dispositionally empathetic we are, the difference between low and high empathy, and practices that can help you develop your empathic skills.

Lessons

1. Recognition is the first education.

2. Wounds and trauma can be passed down from generation to generation.

3. Avoidance, deprivation, over-reactivity, and passive aggression are defenses that people carry sometimes for the rest of their lives.

4. People who avoid feelings live an overintellectualized life.

5. Emotions come in a continuous flow, not as discrete events.

6. Having defensive methods is not bad but you have to be careful because it can control you.

7. A defensive system built up in childhood can limit you in adulthood.

8. Communication is the best way to repair your defensive model.

Questions

1. What causes trauma to be transferred to the next generation and how can it be stopped?

_____

_____

_____

_____

_____

_____

_____

_____

_____

2. How can avoidance, deprivation, over-reactivity, and passive aggression prevent you from further trauma or wound?

_____

_____

_____

_____

_____

_____

_____

_____

_____

_____

_____

3. Aside family inherited trauma, what other experience can trigger trauma?

_____

_____

_____

_____

_____

_____

_____

_____

_____

4. How can upbringing define the present plot and trajectory of one's life?

_____

_____

_____

_____

_____

_____

_____

_____

_____

_____

5. What strategy or practices can we use to develop our empathic skills?

_____

_____

_____

_____

_____

_____

_____

_____

_____

_____

_____

_____

6. What sort of problem can arise from using defensive methods like avoidance, deprivation, over-reactivity, and passive aggression?

_____

_____

_____

_____

_____

_____

_____

_____

_____

7. Why is seeing the world through an old model called conceptual blindness?

_____

_____

_____

_____

_____

_____

_____

_____

_____

_____

8. In what way does introspection differ from communication and why is communication better at repairing the defense model?

_____

_____

_____

_____

_____

_____

_____

_____

_____

9. Why is empathy necessary when we are accompanying someone who is wrestling with wounds or trauma?

_____

_____

_____

_____

_____

_____

_____

_____

_____

_____

_____

10. What connection does creating emotions have with the body?

_____

_____

_____

_____

_____

_____

_____

_____

_____

_____

CHAPTER TWELVE

How Were You Shaped by Your Sufferings?

Objectives

1. To recognize that suffering can shape your future.

2. To explore the possibility of remaking and reinterpreting our story.

3. To know what it means to be morally upright.

Summary

The chapter emphasizes the need for us to know who people were before they suffered losses and how they created a new outlook on life if you want to know them better because suffering changes people, how we can help each other reinvent the story of our lives and how we can't cultivate a good character.

Lessons

1. Grief is not a state but a process.

2. To know a person well, you have to know who they were before they suffered their losses and how they remade their whole outlook after them.

3. Grief can be postponed.

4. The more you know of your history, the more liberated you are.

5. Sharing stories and reinterpreting what it means, can help you create new mental models you can use to construct a new reality and a new future.

6. Self-mastery exercises willpower so that you are the master of your passions and not their slave.

7. People need recognition from others if they are to thrive.

8. Virtue is the attempt to pierce the veil of selfish consciousness and join the world as it is.

Questions

1. What is the difference between suffering and grief?

_____

_____

_____

_____

_____

_____

_____

_____

_____

_____

2. Why can it be said that trauma challenges our global meaning system?

_____

_____

_____

_____

_____

_____

_____

_____

_____

3. What is the essence of creating a new model?

_____

_____

_____

_____

_____

_____

_____

_____

_____

_____

4. How do we help each other go back into the past and reinvent the story of our lives?

_____

_____

_____

_____

_____

_____

_____

_____

_____

5. How can sharing and reinterpreting stories help you construct a new reality and future?

_____

_____

_____

_____

_____

_____

_____

_____

_____

_____

6. What exactly does it mean to be a morally upright person?

_____

_____

_____

_____

_____

_____

_____

_____

_____

_____

7. How can we cultivate a good character and be morally better?

_____

_____

_____

_____

_____

_____

_____

_____

_____

_____

8. Why is self-mastery important in the process of cultivating a good character?

_____

_____

_____

_____

_____

_____

_____

_____

_____

_____

9. Why are one's social interaction skills more important than his willpower?

_____

_____

_____

_____

_____

_____

_____

_____

_____

10. How has your suffering shaped you?

_____

_____

_____

_____

PART 3

I SEE YOU WITH YOUR STRENGTH

CHAPTER THIRTEEN

Personality: What Energy Do You Bring into the Room?

Objectives

1. To understand how personality can shape the future.

2. To educate readers on how to identify personality traits.

3. To understand the connection between personality traits and how you see someone.

Summary

This chapter delves into personality and how it can shape your future in a good or bad way like George Washington Bush. It highlights the Big Five traits (extroversion, conscientiousness, neuroticism, agreeableness, and openness) which can be used to measure personality traits, their advantages and disadvantages. It further highlights the advantage of the Big Five traits over the Myers-Briggs questionnaire.

Lessons

1. Your personality trait can either shape your life in a good or bad way.

2. If you want to understand another person, you have to be able to describe the particular energy they bring into a room.

3. A personality trait is a habitual way of seeing, interpreting, and reacting to a situation.

4. Extroverts are motivated more by the lure of rewards than the fear of punishment.

5. Extroverts live their lives as high-reward/high-risk exercise.

6. Conscientiousness is discipline, persevering, organized, and self-regulating. They can focus on long-term goals and not get distracted.

7. People with high neuroticism are drawn to negative emotions while extroverts are drawn to positive emotions.

8. Personality traits are not only gifts they are gifts you can build over your lifetime.

Questions

1. How do our personality traits shape our future?

_____

_____

_____

_____

_____

_____

_____

_____

2. What is the difference between Big Five traits and the Myers-Briggs questionnaire?

_____

_____

_____

_____

_____

_____

_____

_____

_____

3. What advantage do the Big Five traits have over the Myers-Briggs questionnaire?

_____

_____

_____

_____

_____

_____

_____

_____

_____

4. What are the advantages and disadvantages of extroversion?

_____

_____

_____

_____

_____

_____

_____

_____

_____

_____

_____

5.   How   is   extroversion   advantageous   over
conscientiousness?

_____

_____

_____

_____

_____

_____

_____

_____

_____

6. Of what significance are our personality traits to our
present and future life?

_____

_____

_____

_____

_____

_____

_____

_____

_____

_____

_____

_____

7. Why are neurotics drawn to negative emotions and extrovert's positive emotions?

_____

_____

_____

_____

_____

_____

_____

_____

_____

_____

8. Is it possible for one to change his personality trait, if yes, what challenge are you likely to face doing the process?

_____

_____

_____

_____

_____

_____

_____

_____

_____

9. From your point of view, what is the difference between agreeableness and openness as mentioned in the chapter?

_____

_____

_____

_____

_____

_____

_____

10. How can we rate the Big Five traits?

CHAPTER FOURTEEN

Life Tasks

Objectives

1. To shed light on the need to understand the life task that a person is in.

2. To explore the various types and stages of life tasks.

3. To be able to identify our life tasks and that of others.

Summary

This chapter delves into the various life tasks we have (starting from when we were a baby with our first task being to bond with the person who will feed and care for them) with the states of consciousness that arise to help us meet each one of those tasks. It also emphasizes the need for us to know the life task a person is in, if we want to know the person better.

Lessons

1. Adults have spotlight consciousness while babies have lantern consciousness.

2. A person has to either display industry or succumb to inferiority.

3. Imperial consciousness occurs in children and teenagers but can sometimes be cared for to adulthood.

4. A person with an interpersonal consciousness is more likely to describe herself according to her psychological traits.

5. Each new life task requires a different level of consciousness.

6. During career consolation, intimacy motivation takes a step back and achievement motivation takes a step forward.

7. Career success does not satisfy.

8. A generative person gives others the gift of admiration, seeing them for the precious creatures they are.

Questions

1. How is the consciousness of an adult different from that of a baby?

_____

_____

_____

_____

_____

_____

_____

_____

_____

_____

_____

2. How do we identify the life task that a person is in?

_____

_____

_____

_____

_____

_____

_____

_____

_____

3. What is the connection between development physiology and life task?

_____

_____

_____

_____

_____

_____

_____

_____

_____

_____

_____

4. Why is it important to know and understand life tasks?

_____

_____

_____

_____

_____

_____

_____

_____

_____

_____

_____

_____

5. What strategy can you use to display yourself so as not to succumb to inferiority?

_____

_____

_____

_____

_____

_____

_____

_____

_____

6. According to this chapter, how can you relate imperial tasks with imperial consciousness?

_____

_____

_____

_____

_____

_____

_____

_____

_____

_____

7. What is the difference between imperial and interpersonal consciousness?

_____

_____

_____

_____

_____

_____

_____

_____

_____

8. What is the difference between the various types of life tasks mentioned in this chapter?

_____

_____

_____

_____

_____

_____

_____

_____

_____

_____

_____

9. How do identifying the life tasks of people help us know them better?

_____

_____

_____

_____

_____

_____

_____

_____

_____

10. After reading this chapter, which stage of life task are you in?

_____

_____

CHAPTER FIFTEEN

Life Stories

Objectives

1. To know the benefit of social connection and sharing your life story.

2. To know the various modes of thinking.

3. To educate the reader on how to ask questions about the life stories of others, what to think when listening to the life stories of others, and how to identify if the story is true.

Summary

This chapter highlights the importance of sharing your life stories with others and social connection as it brings you happiness. It talks about the various modes of thinking, how society has more paradigmatic thinkers than narrative thinkers, how to shift paradigmatic story mode to narrative story mode, the right questions to ask and what to think while listening to the story of others, the wonders of the inner voice and how it is different in each person.

Lessons

1. Social connection is the number one source of happiness, success, and good health.

2. There are two different modes of thinking which are the paradigmatic mode and the narrative mode.

3. The paradigmatic mode is a mental state that involves amassing data, collecting evidence, and offering hypotheses.

4. Narrative mode involves understanding the unique individuals in front of us.

5. We live in a culture that is paradigmatic rich and narrative poor.

6. What you do for a living shapes you into who you become.

7. The inner voice is one of the greatest miracles in all nature.

8. By listening to other people's stories you are helping them to create more stories.

Questions

1. Why is social connection significant to humans?

_____

_____

_____

_____

_____

_____

_____

_____

_____

_____

_____

2. Why are people not doing things that make them the happiest?

_____

_____

_____

_____

_____

_____

_____

_____

_____

_____

3. What advantage do storytelling conversations have over comment-making conversations?

_____

_____

_____

_____

_____

_____

_____

_____

_____

_____

4. How does the paradigmatic mode of thinking differ from the narrative mode of thinking?

_____

_____

_____

_____

_____

_____

_____

_____

_____

_____

_____

5. How can we improve the narrative thinking of our society?

_____

_____

_____

_____

_____

_____

_____

_____

6. Why is it said that our culture is paradigmatic rich and narrative poor?

_____

_____

_____

_____

_____

_____

_____

_____

_____

_____

_____

7. How can you shift a conversation from paradigmatic mode to narrative mode?

_____

_____

_____

_____

_____

_____

_____

_____

_____

_____

_____

8. From your perspective, what are the right questions to ask someone for him or her to tell you their life stories?

_____

_____

_____

_____

_____

_____

_____

_____

_____

9. What questions should you ask yourself when listening to the life stories of others and how can you identify that those stories are true?

_____

_____

_____

_____

_____

_____

_____

_____

_____

_____

10. Why is it said that calm is a function of retrospective clarification?

_____

_____

_____

_____

_____

_____

_____

_____

_____

_____

_____

_____

_____

_____

_____

CHAPTER SIXTEEN

How Do Your Ancestors Show Up in Your Life?

Objectives

1. To recognize and acknowledge the legacy felt by our ancestors.

2. To understand what culture is and correct some of the misconceptions about culture.

3. To emphasize the past and how the dead live in us.

Summary

This chapter talks about the importance of the legacy felt by our ancestors and how we have to value it for us to move forward in life. It condemns the present grouping of people (black/white, gay/straight, Republican/Democrat). It further talks about culture, some misconceptions of culture, and how culture varies from place to place. It also emphasizes the role of our ancestors in making the world what it is today.

Lessons

1. We live our childhoods at least twice. First, we live through them with eyes of wonderment, and then later in

life, we have to revisit them to understand what it all meant.

2. People who don't look back to their ancestors will not look forward to posterity.

3. Your consciousness is formed by the choices of your ancestors.

4. Culture is not everything and it is not nothing.

5. To see a person well, you have to see them as culture inheritors and as culture creators.

6. Culture is a shared symbolic landscape that we use to construct our reality.

7. People who grow up in different cultures see the world differently.

8. Insecurities never go away.

Questions

1. What role has your past played in making you who you are today?

_____

_____

_____

_____

_____

_____

_____

_____

_____

_____

2. Why is it significant to look back to our ancestors?

_____

_____

_____

_____

_____

_____

_____

_____

3. How do you see a person as part of your group?

_____

_____

_____

_____

_____

_____

_____

_____

_____

_____

4. Compare a time in your life when you felt mis-seen and where you felt seen, which one was more fulfilling and why?

_____

_____

_____

_____

_____

_____

_____

_____

_____

5. What are some of the misconceptions of culture?

_____

_____

_____

_____

_____

_____

_____

_____

_____

_____

6. Have you ever been in a situation where you wanted to see and understand a person, if yes, what are the challenges you faced?

_____

_____

_____

_____

_____

_____

_____

_____

_____

_____

7. How can we be a culture inheritors and creators?

_____

_____

_____

_____

_____

_____

_____

_____

_____

_____

8. From your point of view, what do you think is the meaning of culture?

_____

_____

_____

_____

_____

_____

_____

_____

_____

_____

_____

9. In what way has your culture impacted your view of the world?

_____

_____

_____

_____

_____

_____

_____

_____

_____

10. In what way has the past or our ancestors impacted the world today?

_____

_____

_____

CHAPTER SEVENTEEN

What Is Wisdom

Objectives

1. To shed light on what wisdom is.

2. To educate the reader on what being wise entails.

3. To prove that is possible to know another person deeply, even a person very different from yourself.

Summary

This chapter highlights the joy you get when you meet someone who truly understands you, what wisdom is, corrects some misconceptions on the definition of wisdom, and how a community of truth is formed. The author also talked about what he has learned so far and how he has put it into practice.

Lessons

1. Wisdom is the ability to see deeply into who people are and how they should move in the complex situations of life.

2. Wise people don't tell others what to do instead they witness your story and help you process your thoughts and emotions.

3. All choices involve loss and reconciling opposites.

4. A wise person creates an atmosphere of hospitality.

5. Not all smart people are wise.

6. Always try to jump at the sun even if we don't reach it, we'll still reach higher than before.

7. Confrontation without receptivity leads to an oppressive aggression that hurts everybody.

8. A community of truth is created when people are genuinely interested in seeing and exploring together.

Questions

1. Have there been a time in your life when you met someone who truly understood you, if yes, how did you feel?

_____

_____

_____

_____

_____

_____

_____

_____

_____

_____

_____

2. After reading this chapter, do you agree with the author's definition of wisdom, if not, then what do you think wisdom is?

_____

_____

_____

_____

_____

_____

_____

_____

_____

3. What are the common misconceptions of wisdom in today's world?

_____

_____

_____

_____

_____

_____

_____

_____

_____

_____

4. What does it mean to be wise?

_____

_____

_____

_____

_____

_____

_____

_____

_____

_____

_____

5. What is the difference and connection between understanding and wisdom?

_____

_____

_____

_____

_____

_____

_____

_____

_____

_____

6. Why is wisdom and understanding significant in our everyday life?

_____

_____

_____

_____

_____

_____

_____

7. How can we relate receptivity to confrontation?

_____

_____

_____

_____

_____

_____

_____

_____

_____

8. How do you see others and be seen by others deeply?

_____

_____

_____

_____

_____

_____

_____

_____

_____

_____

9. After reading this book, what skill do you already practice and what skill do you need to practice?

_____

_____

_____

_____

_____

_____

_____

_____

_____

10. Concerning this book what have you learnt about humanity?

_____

_____

_____

_____

Made in United States
Troutdale, OR
12/01/2024

25629005R00083